Fumio Demura: My Story

ISBN-13: 978-0-692-98215-0

It is my honor to dedicate this book to
my parents, Masu and Hitoshi Demura,
and to my sister, Kinue.

Introduction by Fumio Demura

Often over the years I've considered the idea of writing about my life. My students and many friends and acquaintances have expressed their enthusiastic support for this idea too many times to count. On top of that, I've had a pretty interesting combination of up and down experiences in recent years, including some significant health issues challenging me, an amazing documentary of my life being produced, the city of Santa Ana demolishing our beloved Santa Ana Dojo, and reaching some rather significant anniversaries of teaching and training in martial arts. It's all very astonishing, humbling, and totally unanticipated, and now I'll tell you all about it in this book. By the way, as those of you who know me can tell, yes, a friend provided assistance with transforming my thoughts and stories into words on paper, with the sole purpose of helping me share my story with all of you. Thank you for reading my story.

Chapter 1 – My Family

I will start at the beginning. I was born in Showa 15, in the Japanese equivalent to the year 1940 in the western calendar, and in English my birthday is September 15, 1940. I was born in the town of Onoe-Cho, in the province of Yokohama, in the country of Japan. My parents were Masu and Hitoshi Demura.

My father, Hitoshi Demura, and my mother Masu Demura

After I was born, my parents went on to have many more children. Their next child was my brother Teruo, then our brother Yukio, then our sister Mitsue, then our brother Nobuo, and then our youngest sister Kinue.

This is a very early picture of me

Nobuo   Teruo   Kinue   Fumio   Mitsue   Yukio

Most of my students know my sister Kinue, who has helped me with my household and business matters for much of her life. She and her son, my nephew Kazuya, more generally known as Sean, have lived with me since Sean was born, and together we have created a little family unit that has been an important part of my life.

Before marrying my mother, my father had been married before to a woman who had passed away, and they had two sons, Setsuo and Eiichi, so I started life with two older half-brothers. However, I was the first child, and the first son, the Cho-nan, of the union of my father Hitoshi and my mother Masu, which made me the firstborn son of our family. This is a position of great responsibility in Japanese culture, and I took these responsibilities very seriously. This definitely started me right from the beginning on a path of developing a powerful sense of leadership and enormous concern for the welfare of people in my care. Of course, as you can imagine, my siblings, older and younger, did not always appreciate my determined spirit in my leadership role, or my energetic approach to anything I consider my responsibility.

Fortunately, my parents taught me what was important in life from very early on. My father always impressed upon me the necessity for and virtues of hard work, so whenever there was anything I felt I needed to accomplish, I've attacked it head on with all the energy needed to achieve the goal. My mother made sure I learned what it means to be a good person, and how to value, understand, and connect with people. She helped me come to understand that the most important thing in life, and my life in particular, is people … not money, not possessions, not accomplishments, not even karate … people. My mother, Masu Demura, is the single most important person in my life.

Thoughts from Kinue Demura

Kinue Demura with her son, Sean, around 1990

When I decided, with my mother's approval, to go and live in the US, my brother, Fumio, petitioned for me to be allowed to come live here.

When I left Japan, my mother told me "You have many siblings in Japan, but your brother Fumio is by himself across the ocean. Someday, when he needs help, you can help."

When my brother became ill a few years ago, my mother's words came to my mind, and I realized "this is the time my mother was talking about 45 years ago."

She was a very wonderful woman.

My father had been a military man, and he was concerned about the effects of World War II on his family. When the US bombed Japan with B-29's in 1944, he moved our family to a new home in a town called Higashi Terao-Machi Tsurimi-Ku at the top of a mountain in Yokohama. This remains my family's home to this day. I treasure my rare visits to my home in Japan. The place where our home had originally been, the place where I was born, was totally destroyed. I strive to have the same kind of wisdom my father showed when he moved our family to a safer place.

As you might guess, after the war we had very little money. We made do in every way, from going barefoot when the weather was warm because we didn't have shoes, to dealing with holes in our shoes when we did have them. We found creative ways to amuse ourselves because we didn't have toys. When I was in elementary school, which was called Higashi-Dai school, many times I would put my little brother on my back and take him with me to school, because we had no money for a baby sitter. Later, when I went to University of Japan Junior High School and High School, my sole transportation was a bicycle, and it got me to school in good weather and bad, in rain and snow.

You may or may not already know that I am particularly fond of fishing – it is one of my very favorite ways to relax, and to spend enjoyable time with family and friends, and of course it brings food to the table. I started fishing when I was growing up, but back then it was only about bringing food to the table – it was never about relaxing or enjoying time with friends. I would spend many long hours catching small fish from the river near my home, and I'd bring the fish home for my mother to cook for us – fishing was an important part of helping to feed our family.

There was another way, a more unusual way, that I brought food to our family. Near our home was a farm, a rice field. I would go to that rice field and spend all night catching grasshoppers – yes, grasshoppers – and my mother cooked those grasshoppers for us to eat. Nowadays it's considered to be very new and exciting to eat things like grasshoppers. Back then it wasn't at all new or exciting … it was what we needed to do to live.

Another part of being frugal, of needing to take care of our needs with our own effort, became apparent when my father fell ill with heart disease. I was a teenager at that time, and I learned to tend him during his illness, each day giving him therapeutic massage and other care that he needed. I did this, not just because it saved money, but because I considered it my responsibility, and my honor, to do these things for my father.

My efforts to provide for our family defined my high school years. After my father passed away, it became my most important role to help my mother in every way I could. When I was around 17-18 years old, I had three different jobs at the same time – I loaded and unloaded boats in the harbor, I sold fruit in a local fruit store, and I delivered ice – just like in the US, back then many households did not have a refrigerator at home, and they depended on deliveries of ice to keep food cold. There were also times when I added delivering newspapers at 3am in the morning, cleaning floors as a janitor, and working in people's gardens. Everything I earned from all of this work I gave to my mother, to help her provide for our family.

While I was working so many jobs, it was very difficult to get in my schooling. My best friend, Isamu Nishiki, was in much the same situation, and we'd help each other sneak out of school and cover for each other so that we could work as much as possible. Isamu was gifted in the arts and attended special classes for drama and dancing in addition to his regular classes. He was my best friend from childhood until his death in 2011.

Isamu, standing behind me, and I were always best friends.

Other members of Isamu's family have always been and still are very important to me personally, and they have also been involved in my organization. His wife, Kiyoe, once came and demonstrated traditional Japanese dancing at one of our tournaments. His brother,

Minoru, was deeply involved in our group's sword training – much more on that later. His son, Ken, is today one of our valued instructors.

Growing up this way helped me understand the importance of being frugal, of not wasting anything. I save everything I can, because it will be needed and useful for a future purpose. Even old magazine pages can be made into origami birds that give little moments of joy to the people around us – and people who know me well know that making and sharing Japanese origami cranes (Tsuru) is a special pastime that means a great deal to me. I won't say I enjoyed the many hardships my family faced, but I can say that they helped me appreciate the large and small riches in my life, then and now.

I did manage to graduate high school, even with all of my responsibilities. After graduation, I attended Nihon (Japan) University, where I studied economics. I had to attend night classes, because day classes were too expensive. At that time I worked in the warehouse of a pharmaceuticals company, earning the US equivalent of $360 per month. Right about that same time was also when big things started happening in my life, as you will read farther on, and the direction of my life changed completely – in other words, and as you already know, I did not become an economist, and I did not keep working for the pharmaceuticals company.

You might be wondering if it was always peaceful in my family. However, much like every other family, we had our problems and disagreements. One very big disagreement happened around 1962 when one of my half-brothers sued me for insurance fraud. After my father died, there was some money from insurance in an account at the bank. When I was trying to start my own life as an adult, my mother wanted to help me by letting me use some of the insurance money. When my half-brother heard about this, he sued me, and in court won his case against me. Luckily, I was able to take him back to court a second time, and I won that time, but I had to pay a lot of money. In today's society we hear about family feuds and lawsuits all the time, and I know exactly how it feels to experience something like that. Fortunately, over time, we got over our disagreement, and over the lawsuit … and I know that I am very lucky, because many families never do recover from these kinds of things.

By the way, you may not know this, but at that time in Japan handwritten signatures were not used. We used individualized stamps, even for important transactions at the bank. My mother let me use the stamp of my father, and it carried the same weight as if he had actually signed for the bank transaction. My students have always seen me using stamps alongside my signature on certificates and special letters, but they may not know even now that it isn't just a matter of style or wanting to appear important. It is something I do deliberately because it is meaningful.

Chapter 2 – Martial Arts, My Early Years

When I was about eight years old, my mother decided I needed something healthy to do. One of our neighbors, Mr. Asano, knew kendo, and I asked him if I could take lessons from him. When he agreed to teach me, my father cut down a small tree and shaped a bokken, a wooden practice sword, for me to train with. I had never done anything in martial arts before, but as you have probably guessed this soon became my passion, and each day I eagerly ran home to do my kendo training.

My next step, one that ended up being one of the most important steps along my path in martial arts training, happened when our neighbor moved away. Before leaving, he introduced me to a new kendo teacher, Mr. Ryusho Sakagami, the man who would become my Sensei, and who would have the greatest impact of any person in my martial arts life. He taught me about karate and about all of the many different things I needed to know to become a leader of a dojo and an organization. My students know what I mean when I say that Ryushi Sakagami was my Sensei.

Mr. Sakagami, on the left, was my Sensei.

In the beginning, though, we did not know what the future held. Mr. Sakagami just continued my kendo training – I was still just a kid, and he didn't have any other plans for me at that point. However, after I finished kendo each day, I would hang around and watch the next class he taught, which was a karate class. At that time, at least in Mr. Sakagami's dojo, karate training was just for adults. I would watch the classes, hungry with desire to participate, but Mr.

Sakagami didn't take me seriously at all in the beginning. Interestingly, it was his wife, Mrs. Sakagami, who really noticed my growing desire. I don't know what she said, but I know she talked to her husband, because one day he asked me if I was really interested in karate training. Thankfully, when I told him I was very interested, he believed me, and he let me join the class even though I was much younger than the other students, and I started my amazing karate journey that continues to this day.

Training in karate was my all-consuming passion. I was often still at the dojo when midnight came. I remember when Mr. Sakagami would tell me to go home, because I made his electric bill too high! I think his food bill must have been too high, too, because Mrs. Sakagami would usually feed me dinner before I would leave for the night.

At that time in our town, children had a 10 pm curfew. There was a local policeman who used to stop me and give me a rough time if he found me making my way home at midnight. Fortunately, after a while he seemed to get to like me a bit, because he stopped bothering me when he saw me. That made things easier for me, because I wasn't going to stop training those long hours just because the police didn't like it! (Of course, today I always tell kids to obey the law and stay out of trouble, but that was a different time for me.)

It took me four years to become a Black Belt, and this path was one of the hardest in my life. I was not a natural at karate – I had to work HARD! At first I thought I was training well enough, but I had an overconfident opinion of my skills. I failed my very first kyu test for eighth kyu. I was totally horrified! I became completely determined that I would never fail again. Whenever I had a test ahead of me, I trained and trained and trained, making each technique, each kata, my response to each command, as perfect as I could make it. I have never failed another test. More importantly, I have always kept that same attitude of striving for perfection, and it has helped me acquire the expertise and body of knowledge that I have been fortunate to develop, and that I can now share with my students.

I have had some students apply themselves with such determination, but I do wish that more students would strive to actually perfect their understanding and technique, as opposed to just thinking that's what they are doing. It's not about passing tests, or winning tournaments … it is about experiencing the rewards of hard work, and about achieving the greatest level of expertise and knowledge possible for you. I've known some students whose bodies are especially well-suited for jumping high, or moving with exceptional speed or strength, or demonstrating eye-popping flexibility – interestingly enough such students often do not reach their true potential, because it is all so easy for them. On the other hand, I've known students whose bodies are just not that good at performing the techniques of karate, but through extreme dedication to training and attempting always to perfect technique, they achieved a level of ability and understanding beyond their dreams. These students that had to work harder have often become our most capable instructors.

Chapter 3 – Beginnings With Kendo, Iai-Do, Kobudo

Although I had started on my path to becoming a master of karate, at the same time I was also experiencing some amazing opportunities in kendo and kobudo training, as well. Mr. Sakagami knew Masters who were experts in these disciplines, and because they respected him, they generously agreed to let me train with them.

For example, Mr. Taizaburo Nakamura came to Mr. Sakagami's dojo for a time while I was training there. Today Mr. Nakamura is one of the most acclaimed of all Batto-Do Masters, but when I first met him, he was not yet famous. It was an enormous benefit to receive kendo training from this amazingly knowledgeable sword Master. Later I'll share more about the powerful effect Mr. Nakamura had on my life and the growth in martial arts through our amazing relationship that started in that dojo so many years ago.

Another powerful Master I came to know during my early training was Mr. Shinken Taira. He also came for a time in Mr. Sakagami's dojo. Although he was not well-known back when I first knew him, today Mr. Taira is recognized as one of the original leaders in kobudo expertise, the Master who created so much of the development of weapons technique, kata, and application. Mr. Taira was responsible for introducing me to Okinawan kobudo weapons and, he trained me extensively. Again, this humble beginning would have far reaching effects in my martial arts life that continue to evolve even now, and I will talk much more about that later, as well.

After I had been with Mr. Sakagami for about ten years, he decided I was ready to start training in Iai-Do, in the Eishin-Ryu style. Iai-Do is primarily about drawing a sword and performing kata with it.

My first sword studies were in the art of Iai-Do.

The sword holds a special place throughout Japanese culture. There is a great deal of discipline and attention to very specific detail involved in this art, and it added a sense of formality and elegance to my understanding of martial arts. This was yet another of the many ways in which Mr. Sakagami shaped and directed my development as a martial artist.

Chapter 4 – My Emergence in the World of Karate

In Showa 34, which is 1958 in the western calendar, the Japan
Karate Association had the very first all-Japan karate tournament.
This was a very exciting development, although this tournament was
just for the Shotokan style, and didn't include all of the other
Japanese karate styles. My style was (and still is, of course) Shito-
Ryu, but that didn't diminish my interest. I went to the tournament
and sat in the audience to watch and learn everything I could, and I
was totally fascinated with everything I saw. The kumite
competition was like nothing I had ever seen before. I immediately
went back to Mr. Sakagami's dojo and started training intensively
for tournament fighting.

Three years later, in 1961, the Japan Karate Federation had their first
all-Japan tournament, and their tournament included all Japanese
karate styles for the very first time. Each Japanese province could
only send two competitors, and I was one of the students
representing Yokohama. Not all provinces had people to send, but

there were still about 80 competitors – all of them top Black Belts from all over Japan. Over 16,000 people came to watch the tournament and saw me become the first All-Japan Kumite Champion. At that moment, my life changed forever.

Trophies I won.

Me with my certificate of first place in kumite.

After I won the tournament, when I returned to the dojo Mr. Sakagami gave me his classes to teach. Officially becoming an instructor began another new phase in my martial arts development, and this new phase brought a great many challenges for me. Right from the beginning, Mr. Sakagami would argue with me because I did not teach the way he did. Early on, though, I understood instinctively that the way a person teaches is a very individual thing, and eventually Mr. Sakagami came to see that, as well.

My ongoing intensive training, in addition to becoming an instructor, was allowing me to develop quickly as a martial artist with a broad and deep body of expertise. In 1962, a year after winning the All-Japan Tournament, I was involved in a kobudo demonstration and exhibition in Tokyo as Mr. Sakagami's assistant. In the same exhibition, Mr. Donn Draeger, a well-known martial artist from the United States, was also participating with his demonstration of Jo-Do. Mr. Draeger and I became acquainted, and he created the next very critical step in my career by introducing me to Mr. Dan Ivan. Everyone who knows me knows that it was Dan Ivan who was responsible for bringing me to America.

Me with Donn Draeger.   *Dan Ivan with his son, Doug.*

When I first knew Dan Ivan, our relationship consisted mostly of me

teaching him the sai every day while he was in Japan. My abilities

in martial arts and as an instructor impressed Dan, and it wasn't long

before he asked me if I was interested in coming to the United States

to teach karate. I actually said no the first time he asked, because

this wasn't long after President Kennedy had been assassinated, and

my family was very concerned that it wouldn't be safe for me to go

there, but Dan persisted.

[Throughout this book, I refer to different weapons. I know some of

my readers may not know what these weapons look like, so at the

end of the book is a set of pictures so you can see what the weapons

are called and what they look like.]

Chapter 5 – My Beginnings in America

Okay, we all know I eventually said yes, and in 1965 I did indeed come to America.

I was excited to come to America.

Yes, it was exciting, but it really wasn't what you'd call fun at first. Talk about challenges! Teaching karate is hard enough, but add to that a complete language change and a massive culture change … I'll try to give you an idea of how things went.

Dan already had a small karate school in California, in Orange County, so I was able to start teaching immediately. I stayed in Dan's house, and fortunately his wife was Japanese, or I wouldn't have had anybody to talk to at all. I hadn't anticipated just how hard it would be to be dropped into a place where virtually nobody spoke Japanese, and then have to learn English on the fly. English is considered the hardest language to learn to speak, and I can tell you from experience that it is. I was totally overwhelmed, and I admit that I came very close to running back to Japan as fast as my feet could carry me, with or without a boat! However, I have a strong personal rule that I do not run away from challenges. I kept working, teaching, and learning, and I finally started making headway.

Right away, one of my very first students was a young man who had a white belt with two stripes, and what looked to me like a Japanese face. I was delighted to find a Japanese person to talk to, and ran up to him and started a rapid-fire conversation in Japanese. Dan Ivan came running up to us and quickly told me that the poor guy was a Native American who didn't know any Japanese at all! I can only imagine how the poor guy felt at that moment – he was only a white belt, which is scary enough all by itself, and here comes the new Master from Japan running up and talking as fast as lightning in his face. Now, after all these years, Dwight Lomayesva is still my student, the longest of all my students, and a valued friend and colleague. Of course, Dwight loves telling the story of how we met!

Thoughts from Dwight Lomayesva

Dwight Lomayesva, left, and Sensei Demura at a Genbu-Kai tournament

When I first met Sensei Demura, I was very impressed with his ability to spar with our senior students, some of whom were tall, quick, and very skilled. As I attended classes, I became more impressed with his teaching skills and his charismatic ability to captivate the audience in demonstrations. This was very apparent when he did demonstrations at the Japanese Village. I was not surprised when he was voted into the Black Belt Hall of fame within five years after he arrived in the United States. Throughout the fifty plus years that I have trained with Sensei Demura, I found that another great asset he has is his skills as an organizational leader. Under his leadership, Genbu-Kai has grown and flourished, and his students have made a positive impact on their communities and in the world of martial arts. One of my fondest memories is the time we worked together to produce a martial arts expo to raise food for the hungry in our community.

My first junior class only had about five or six kids in it. Teaching karate to kids was, and still is today, one of the most frustrating, enjoyable, baffling, and rewarding experiences I've ever known. One of those first junior students was a seven year old boy named David Hines. I've essentially known Dave his entire life, and he has been my student all this time. Now he is one of our most valued instructors, and one of my right-hand people, responsible for a great deal of the work of running our organization.

Thoughts from Dave Hines

David Hines

I have known Sensei Demura since I was seven, and he has been involved in my in life in some way or another ever since. He has seen me grow through all of the phases of my schooling, from elementary school through college. He was there when I got married. He watched my two boys grow up in the dojo from when they were 2 weeks old. He taught my children about karate and about life. In many ways he knows me as well as my parents, in some ways maybe even better. Knowing Sensei all these years has been one of the most amazing experiences of my life. My family and I are lucky and will always appreciate everything Sensei has taught us.

Soon after I arrived, Dan Ivan moved his school to a house he rented on 17th Street in Santa Ana. The house had a garage, where we held the classes. In the house we had two or three beds, one of which was mine. Outside of teaching, there wasn't much to do at first. On weekends, I would sit on the porch and watch the cars go by. During this early time, my frugal upbringing served me well. Dan Ivan was paying me $100 per month, and of that I was sending $80 home to my mother, and living on $20 per month. Even for the 60's, that was some pretty frugal living.

Of course I couldn't read English, which created some interesting situations. Numbers were easy, so when I went to the market to buy food, I could read prices, but I couldn't read labels. I found some canned meat-type food that was the cheapest thing they sold. After a few days, one of my students asked me where my cat was, which confused me. It turned out he had noticed in my trash can a lot of empty cat food cans! Well, at least it actually tasted pretty good.

There were some pretty big cultural differences, too. Now, you may already know that a traditional Japanese toilet is essentially a hole in the floor. Many of my students know my story of my first experience with a western toilet. Honestly, it looked to me like a seat with a little desk, perfect for reading magazines while sitting there. I accidentally walked in on someone else using the bathroom, though, and was shocked to see them facing the other direction… it turned out I was sitting on the thing backwards!

That particular cultural difference also worked going the other direction. One of the first times I brought Americans with me to visit Japan, one of them slipped and sat directly down in the hole of the toilet in the floor, and his behind got stuck in it. He called for help, and I pulled him out of the toilet, and then I hung a rope from the doorknob so my American visitors could have a little help balancing. If an American visitor was too long in the bathroom, though, my mother would always knock on the door and ask if they were okay, just in case.

When my mother came to visit me in America, and went into the bathroom for the first time, I didn't even think to warn her about the difference. She came running out and told me that western toilets were too dangerous to use. She had tried to climb up on the seat and balance on it to put her feet near the opening like she would have at home! I was very glad she did not hurt herself! After she got used to it, though, my mother liked the western toilet much more than the Japanese toilet, and it wasn't long before she had one installed in our home in Japan.

My mother once came to visit me for her birthday,
which I enjoyed very much!

I started meeting interesting people right from the beginning of my new life in America, some of whom became very important to me over the years. One such person was a unique character known as "The Great John L" who was an actor, professional wrestler, and stuntman that Dan Ivan knew. He liked me immediately and became a kind of American father to me, and we remained close until he passed away in 2005. John L was responsible for getting me started on some of my many adventures, as you will later read.

As all of these different experiences were unfolding, I also came very close to getting drafted into the US army and sent to Vietnam. This was around 1968, and back then if you lived in the US for more than three months, you were eligible for the draft. The government actually started putting me through the drafting process, and I even had to go to Long Beach for my military physical. Luckily several things worked to keep me out of the infantry. One thing was that, even though I was in excellent physical shape, I was a bit older than other guys also eligible for the draft at that time. Another was that my number was way down the list. For those of you who are too young to know, back then men had to register for the draft, and when they did they received a number, and luckily mine was a long way from being called. I was very fortunate that they did not call my number before the war ended in 1973. However, I did remain in the army reserves, and could have possibly been called into service, for many years after that.

Chapter 6 – Inspiration and Opportunities

When I first started teaching in Dan's school, he was teaching the style of Shotokan karate. Karate was still considered somewhat exotic in regular American culture, but within karate schools in America, Shotokan was probably one of the most widely taught styles at that time. Of course I knew Shotokan karate, and all of the other Japanese styles of karate, as well, so I did not have any trouble teaching. However, the style I learned from Mr. Sakagami was Shito-Ryu. I knew I wanted to teach my new students Shito-Ryu, but I had to take my time. Slowly over the years I introduced Shito-Ryu to my students, as well as to the American martial arts scene. Before long, my organization became known as training in the style of Shito-Ryu. Since then, I have seen many other schools come after me to also start teaching in this style, and now Shito-Ryu is taught by many organizations in America.

In the early days, I was teaching four classes every day, five days a week, so even if I had been making a lot of money, I wouldn't have had the time or energy to do much with it. The classes weren't terribly large at first, but they were big enough to have a good school, and we slowly gathered more and more students.

At the same time, I was also creating opportunities and making connections, and having experiences that were amazing and productive. So many times I would establish a relationship with a person or organization, and it would lead to another person, another opportunity, sometimes sooner, sometimes coming back to make a connection many years later.

One of my first amazing adventures happened soon after I arrived in 1965, when one of my students, Richard Fujitani, took me to Knott's Berry Farm for the first time. Many of you already know about the old west train ride at Knott's, and about the train robbery show they would put on for people riding the train, but I had no idea that was going to happen. When the train robbers came in and pretended to rob us, I immediately jumped up and disarmed the robber of what looked to me like a real gun – which was a total surprise to him! Richard had to quickly reassure me that we weren't in any danger, and even more importantly he had to reassure the robber that he wasn't in any danger, either!

I took some of my first steps into the limelight when I went to Ed Parker's International Karate Championships in Long Beach, California, where I did a demonstration of the sai that was enormously well received. Another attendee at that tournament was Chuck Norris, and we met and established a bond immediately. Chuck would visit my dojo where he trained with me many times. I also met many of Chuck's students, including one named Pat Johnson – more about Mr. Johnson, later.

I also started developing relationships with law enforcement. Some of my students have been in law enforcement, and through them, I have often been asked to give self defense seminars to police departments. Some of the seminars were in the use of police batons that were very similar to the tonfa, one of our kobudo weapons. I was very glad to be able to contribute to society in this specific area. It is important for our law enforcement to effectively protect themselves without unnecessarily harming people they must deal with. I showed them ways to help them do their jobs effectively, and I hope this prevented injuries for many people.

In 1968, there was a competition for California Police Olympics being held at Santa Ana College, and I was asked to help with their tournament. This lead to two very special jobs for me – Director of karate competition for the Annual California Police Olympic Games, and also for the Annual World Police and Fire Olympic Games. As you might guess, the competitors at these events, being policemen and firemen, were powerful, physical, and very driven. I remember, early on, watching one competitor deliver a backhand that made hard contact and gave his opponent a very bloody and badly broken nose. Safety was not always a priority with these fighters. It was my job to create an environment that both protected competitors from injury and at the same time allowed them to compete with their natural power and energy. I did these jobs for over 35 years, I believe largely successfully – this work was very important to me.

I must mention my time at Japanese Village, in Buena Park, California, where I performed from 1970-74. This was the place where I first started really developing the idea of improving demonstrations of Japanese martial arts for the public to experience and enjoy.

It all started when a friend took me to Japanese Village and Deer Park. We bought deer food for ten cents and spent a lovely time walking around the beautiful grounds. Then we went inside to watch a demonstration of Japanese dancing and see some of the other shows and exhibits they put on. It was interesting and pretty, but at that time I didn't think anything more about it.

Then came one of those interesting connections that bring amazing opportunities in life. Some time after our visit to Japanese Village, one of their managers became one of my students. He immediately saw that there was great potential for Japanese Village to benefit from having us do Japanese martial arts demonstrations as part of their culture show, and I immediately saw that there was great potential for me to gain exposure and presence in martial arts and in entertainment. I didn't even care how much money they paid – I just wanted to get on that stage and start working toward a new future for martial arts.

At first we did shows only on Saturday and Sunday, but people loved the shows, and the crowds were so big that customers started complaining that they couldn't see. The following summer, management decided to let us do more, and we started performing Monday through Friday, two shows a day, five days a week. I noticed, though, that while people definitely wanted to watch us, they didn't have much reaction during the performance. That's when I really started changing things – I wanted the crowd to be absolutely thrilled, amazed, and excited.

First, we stopped just doing stiff demonstrations of techniques, and added more exciting choreography. We started making it look like we were really fighting, with fast attacks and defenses, and a lot of action, shouting, and people flying back from being "hit" by attackers. The crowd loved it! Then we added costumes, music, and weapons, and the crowd really went wild! We were a big success, the top show in Japanese Village. Soon we were looking for more people to bring in to the demonstrations, and we found some talented young men, such as Doug Ivan (Dan's son), Sho Kosugi, Hiroshi Ikushima, Kyoshi Yamazaki, and Steven Seagal. Those names are now very familiar in the martial arts world, and of course Steven Seagal has become a famous actor, but in those days we were just getting started, and Japanese Village was an important early step for all of us.

Steven Seagal and I have known each other for a long time.

Before our big breakthrough at Japanese Village, demonstrations of martial arts were kind of, well, boring. I wanted to make them more realistic, more interesting and exciting. It took some doing – I met with a lot of resistance from both the martial arts and entertainment establishments. Fortunately, as I mentioned before, I do not quit in the face of a challenge. I knew this was the new, best direction for martial arts, and I pushed until I made my point, and once that door was opened, it never closed again.

One of the people I needed to convince early on was Mr. Sakagami. When he heard rumors about the changes I was making to the way I did demonstrations, he did not approve at first. I asked him to come visit me and see what I was doing for himself. When he came it was during our annual tournament and I did one of my demonstrations. I was nervous and excited – I wanted him to understand what I was trying to accomplish. Mr. Sakagami saw how effective the demonstration was and how the audience reacted with excitement and interest. He gave me his approval, which meant a great deal to me, and his support gave me even more confidence to continue my work, my passion.

Did you know I had a Las Vegas act? As it turned out, the big oil crisis in 1973 hit Japanese Village very hard, and in 1974 they closed down their operation, including our demonstrations. Literally something like two days later, I got a call from the Las Vegas Hilton asking me to come and do an audition. I brought along some of my students, such as Doug Ivan, Liz and Dave Javier, and Steven

Ambuter. Kyoshi Yamazaki was part of our team at first, but shortly

after that he parted ways with Dan Ivan and started his own karate

group.

From 1974 through 1976 the act went on at the Las Vegas Hilton

with six shows a night, six days a week, from Tuesday through

Sunday, with only Mondays off. My team performed without me

Tuesday through Thursday, but I drove out each Friday to join the

demonstrations Friday through Sunday, and at 1am each Monday

morning (as in right after midnight Sunday night) I would head back

to Orange County. Often, some of my Santa Ana students would

come along with me if they could, and they would participate in our

demonstrations. That was how I always approached our act, as

another powerful, exciting martial arts demonstration.

Las Vegas was where I originally met Pat Morita – he used to be a

stand-up comedian and was associated with Redd Foxx. I also knew

Engelbert Humperdink, Priscilla Presley, and many other

entertainment celebrities. I became friends with Rocky Aoki, the owner of the Benihana Lounge in the Hilton, where our demonstrations were staged. Once, Wayne Newton was putting on a charitable event and invited us to participate with a demonstration. We became good friends, and I still often go to Wayne's house in Las Vegas to celebrate his birthday.

Many other relationships also grew from the Japanese Village years. After Japanese Village closed, the people who were part of that organization went to join many other entertainment establishments in Southern California, such as Magic Mountain, Knott's Berry Farm, and The Queen Mary. I kept my relationships with those people, and was able to create many more new opportunities with them in their new organizations.

I added a new dimension when I published my first book in 1971, *Shito-Ryu Karate*. Very quickly that same year I published *Nunchaku: Karate Weapon of Self-Defense*, ultimately my most popular book. Within a few short years, I had written more books on different weapons, including the bo, sai, tonfa, and kama. In later years I wrote many more books on weapons and karate, including

Street Survival, A Practical Guide for Self-Defense, and even today I am still planning more books. As video became more common, I also made many videos about karate and weapons, and likewise hope to make more videos in the future.

For many years, my publisher was Black Belt Communications, also the publisher of the well-respected *Black Belt Magazine*. Many years ago, *Black Belt Magazine* published an article crediting me with bringing kobudo, most especially the nunchaku and sai, to the American people. My process and plans for developing kobudo in this country have continued grow to this day, and I definitely will talk more about that later in this book.

Interestingly, *Nunchaku: Karate Weapon of Self Defense* caught the attention of Bruce Lee, who also had a relationship with Black Belt Communications. After reading my book, Bruce would often meet with me at Black Belt Magazine, and we would have long conversations about martial arts and its ongoing development, and our lives as martial artists. Bruce also asked me to train him in the nunchaku, which he incorporated so successfully in his breakout movie *Enter the Dragon* in 1973.

Steve McQueen, Bruce Lee, and me.

When *Enter The Dragon* came out, that movie helped propel interest in martial arts to unforeseen heights in American culture. Every child in the US wanted to be Bruce Lee, and makeshift nunchaku caused concerns for parents everywhere. Our classes were PACKED!

Chapter 7 – The Santa Ana Dojo

The tidal wave of interest in karate packed our classes to the point that some of our students had to practice in other places. With the money he made from the enormous growth, Dan Ivan bought a house at 1429 N Bristol in Santa Ana. It was just an ordinary house, but we turned it into a dojo, and this became "The" Santa Ana Dojo, where we stayed for more than 40 years. The Santa Ana Dojo became the heart of our entire organization, and the site of countless classes, seminars, tests, and special moments, until it was demolished by the city of Santa Ana in 2016 to help widen Bristol.

This was our home for over 40 years,
our Santa Ana Dojo.

These mats hold countless memories of blood, sweat, and tears.

When we first started working on the dojo, all of our students

helped. People would come and cut lumber, hammer nails, tear

down walls, put up fences – anything that needed doing, we did for

ourselves. It took about a month to turn that house into a dojo with

those early steps. We were always busy, and everybody contributed

their time and energy to create this place and make it ready for class.

I was able to obtain genuine Japanese tatami mats for the workout

floor, which were one of the many beautiful and essential, and of

course very functional, elements that distinguished our dojo.

Over the years we had many students who were plumbers,

electricians, construction workers, woodworkers, and any other kind of capability needed by and for the dojo. It started out and always remained a labor of love to maintain our dojo. An important part of that process was our annual Oosoji, or Dojo Cleaning, done at the end of every year. The whole place was taken apart, cleaned up, and put back together by a group of our students, as we readied ourselves to begin a new year. A big part of this process was taking care of the afore-mentioned tatami mats – we removed, carefully patched and replaced those mats, and made them last as long as the dojo lasted. I can truly say that there was a lot of blood, sweat, and tears soaked into our tatami mats by the time they were retired when we moved to a new location. In truth, after close to 50 years of continuous use, at the end they were literally falling apart beyond all repair. We could fill a book with the memories of our students telling tales of the adventures, joys, and injuries they experienced on those mats!

There were many wonderful traditions we established at that dojo. One of the most vivid and widely shared with the community is the Mochitsuki, or Rice Pounding. Each year, between Christmas and New Year's, we build a fire on some bricks, under a 50 gallon oil drum. Using carefully maintained original Japanese equipment, we steam and then pound rice, and then make mochi, or rice balls, to share with friends and family for good luck in the coming year. This is an ancient Japanese tradition that is not very common any more, at least not in this very fundamental form – but we have kept it as part of our group's karate traditions, and we have held this cherished tradition each year, no matter where the dojo's location was.

I enjoy sharing the art of Mochitzuki with my students.

It has given me great joy to share my Japanese culture with my students. There is great value and beauty in the rich culture in which I was raised. Our martial arts training has included many different styles of Karate-Do, Kobudo, Batto-Do, and Iai-Do, as well as other martial arts from Japan and other places, but there have been so many other things to share, as well. My students have always been eager to learn about things like Mochitsuki, Oosoji, Kangeiko (our annual beach karate training for luck in the new year, which we started doing 48 years ago, and have done every year since), as well as Taiko drumming, Japanese foot massage, Shodo (Japanese calligraphy), traditional cuisine and clothing, and most importantly the elegant courtesies and respectful behaviors that are the essence of Japanese culture. The Santa Ana Dojo was the place where we started sharing these things and making them a permanent part of our lives. The purpose of sharing these many experiences is to be a positive part of the efforts of my students to become good, successful, happy people.

In recent years, I have started teaching calligraphy.

For many years we have developed our Taiko drumming group.

Of course, many wonderful American traditions were also pulled in to become part of our picture, such as our annual Junior Christmas Party, our annual picnic, and many other moments and events we included in our group's cultural growth and development. The dojo was always filled with a glorious combination of Japanese, English, Spanish, and a multitude of other languages spoken by our local students from Orange County, and our students visiting from our schools all over the world, and even including American Sign Language. The Santa Ana Dojo was home to a wonderful combination of cultures that we all continue to carry with us even after leaving that unique and beloved building to history.

Chapter 8 – My Movie Career

As most of you know, I have been in quite a few movies. My first silver screen appearance was in *The Island of Dr. Moreau* with Burt Lancaster in 1977.

*My first movie experience – I'm the short one
standing to the left of film icon Burt Lancaster.*

John L, who I mentioned earlier, was involved with making this movie, and from the beginning he was set to appear in it. He told me I should go audition so I could be in the movie with him, so I did. Even though I could speak a good amount of English by then, my skills did not extend to understanding contracts, so when a fellow

named Brian MacMillan told me to sign a paper and be in the movie,
I just signed the paper. Much to my surprise (and a fair bit of
horror), I found out that I had agreed to fight with lions, tigers, and
bears – literally! Next thing I knew, I was a professional, onscreen
stuntman.

I really did do this fight scene with this tiger, and it was very scary!

Back in those days, safety wasn't quite as big a concern as it is now,
and stunt work could be quite dangerous. I was fighting people and
animals, getting my feet wet literally and figuratively. I don't regret
any of it, but that work involved a lot more sweat, discomfort
(physical and mental), and sheer effort than I could possibly have
anticipated.

My work in *Dr. Moreau* allowed me to join the Screen Actors Guild. After that, for a time I was going to auditions at least weekly. Unfortunately, my English proved to be a problem, and I just couldn't get acting or stunt work. Then my friend Chuck Norris, who was doing well in the movie business, recommended me to Twentieth Century Fox as an instructor for actors who needed to be able to look like they could punch onscreen. This kept me working in the industry.

Chuck and I have remained good friends since we met.

Some time after this, I was asked to read for the part of Mr. Miyagi in a new movie called *The Karate Kid* that was just getting its production started. I read the script and I knew that I did not have the English skills, or the acting skills, to be able to carry off this role successfully, so I told them I did not feel I was the right person to attempt it. Later, they cast Pat Morita for this role – remember, I

knew Pat Morita from my time in Las Vegas.

Thoughts from Pat Johnson

From left to right Pat Johnson, Fumio Demura, Roger Quinland, John Natividad, Monte Bledsoe.

I met Sensei Fumio Demura through Chuck Norris. My first impression was that he was one of the finest gentleman and Martial Artist that I had ever met. His demeanor was one of complete humility and confidence.

Shortly thereafter, I was hired to do a motion picture called *The Karate Kid*. The gentleman that was hired to play Mr. Miyagi, Pat Morita, had no Martial Arts experience at all. When I first read the script, the thought came to me instantly, that this character was really Fumio Demura. When it came time for me to hire a stunt double for Mr. Miyagi, there was no greater choice than Fumio Demura. I had Pat Morita attend Sensei Demura's tournament to observe how a real sensei would conduct himself. From that point on Pat Morita understood how to play the role of Mr. Miyagi.

I knew Sensei Demura as a great Martial Artist through my visits to his National Tournament. Now as our friendship has grown throughout the years, I now know him not just as a great martial artist, but also as a great man whom I consider a close friend.

Also, the stunt coordinator for the film was Pat Johnson, and I already knew Pat Johnson because he was Chuck Norris' student. Pat Johnson recommended that I serve as the stunt and fighting double for Pat Morita. As we worked, Pat Morita modeled much of the characterization of Mr. Miyagi after me. He often humorously referenced our relationship in creating this character in future interviews – fans were sometimes surprised that he could speak perfect English, because he did such a wonderful job of creating Mr. Miyagi's character.

Many of the story elements from the first movie came from my real life, as well. For example, around 1966-68, I owned a Volkswagen, and my junior students would wash my car and they would really do the wax on, wax off technique. Many small details included in the movie about karate training and Japanese culture actually came from my own experiences. I really enjoyed my time spent making *Karate Kid* movies, and I like to think our amazing collaboration contributed something essential to this very special movie.

The two Mr. Miyagi's!
Pat Morita, on the left, patterned much of the character after me.

When *The Karate Kid* came out, it had even more impact on the American public than *Enter the Dragon* had! This movie had such amazing heart, which touched fans of every age, that it created a cultural phenomenon that still ripples through to today. Kids everywhere could relate to the story and the characters, especially Daniel-san, on so many levels. With that movie, interest in martial arts took its most powerful leap ever. Our classes were absolutely filled with people wanting to learn karate, and also wanting to see if they could also experience the heart and soul they saw in the movie. All of this was actually a beautiful fit with our group and our philosophy, and my hopes for all of our students. This phenomenon is something my students are extremely proud of – even today, that movie and that character are some of the first things they mention when they introduce me, and the underlying philosophy continues to remain essential to our teaching and goals.

When *Karate Kid* became such an enormous success, it did a great deal both for Pat Morita and for my own career. Pat starred in a TV series called *Ohara*, and then went on to many other roles in TV and in the movies, and I became his full time stunt double, a role I was happy to fill for 27 years. Of course we also continued our work in the *Karate Kid* movies. I didn't need to do a lot for *Karate Kid II* but I had a great deal to do in the *Karate Kid III* and *The Next Karate Kid*. Over the years, Pat Morita and I developed a wonderful brotherly relationship, with him being an older brother to me, and we remained very close until his death in 2005.

About being a stunt double … yes, it's exciting and interesting … and it's also scary and very dangerous. Do you remember the scene in *Karate Kid III* where Miyagi and Daniel are putting the bonsai tree back in the deep crevasse on the coast? I do – because Ralph Macchio's stunt double and I were hanging from a single rope down the side of that crevasse, and when I accidentally dropped the tree, it fell for a very, very, very long time before hitting the bottom and breaking into a million tiny bits! I asked them to tighten up my rope, but we still needed to do that scene four or five more times – I was so glad when it was over!

I had many opportunities for stunt work excitement. On *Ohara*, once I had to drive a car in a high speed action shot. The part where I had to skid around a turn on purpose went very well, but the part where I accidentally ricocheted off of another car went terribly wrong – luckily only the car got hurt! Another time I had to jump (or was it fall?) off of a 50 foot cliff into the ocean below. Of course, the times I had to fight someone on camera were too many to count. Sometimes I got to be the good guy cop getting to beat up the bad guys, but lots of times I was the bad guy getting beat up. The hardest part was making sure the other guy didn't get hurt!

Making movies let me work with many acting icons. In *The Island of Dr. Moreau*, I worked with classic film star Burt Lancaster. In *The Next Karate Kid*, I worked with Hillary Swank – this was her breakout role – and Michael Ironside. In *Rising Sun*, I was "beaten up" by Sean Connery and Wesley Snipes. Cary Tagawa and I forged a great friendship while working on *Rising Sun* and *Mortal Kombat*. I made lasting friendships with so many wonderful people, such as Lauro Chartrand, Chris Ford, Tamlyn Tomita, Gerald Okumura, John Saxon, Shin Koyamada … I could fill a book with the list of amazing people I've met while working in movies.

Hillary Swank has become one of today's film icons.

I've worked with my good friend Gerald Okumura on many projects.

In Rising Sun I worked with Sean Connery and Wesley Snipes.

Starting from the left, here I am with Tak Kubota, Cary Tagawa, and Tadashi Yamashita in Rising Sun.

Always, though, no matter what kind of adventures I had, my spirit and energy would return to the dojo and teaching my students.

Thoughts from Isaac Florentine

Fumio Demura and Isaac Florentine

I am a movie director. In 2008 I directed a movie titled *Ninja*. The movie was shot in Sofia, Bulgaria, but a part of the movie's story happened in Japan. To me, there was only one person that could create Japan in Bulgaria, and that man was the renowned Karate Sensei Fumio Demura. Sensei Demura willingly agreed to come with a team. I tried to explain to the crew the importance of Sensei - I told them that he is "The Frank Sinatra of Karate". The crew laughed.

A few weeks later we shot a training scene, with a Tonfa vs Bo demo that Demura Sensei performed with his student, Thanh Nguyen. The crew were all seasoned people, but when Sensei and Thanh started moving there was absolute silence. When the demo was over they all clapped with enthusiasm. Tsuyoshi Ihara, a known Japanese actor who starred in the film asked me: "After this Embu how the audience will believe that I am killing such a skillful Master?" The crew came to me and told me "OK, we now understand why you said he's the Frank Sinatra of Karate!'"

I took Sensei and the team (that also included Elisa Au) to tour Sofia, and we went to a little local bakery owned by an elderly Turkish Lady. She didn't speak any English but Sensei folded on the spot a little Origami Crane to give her. The lady beamed with delight and displayed the crane on a shelf. A year later I visited the place and the crane was still sitting on the shelf.

When I started training in karate in the early 70's in my native Israel one of the first books I bought was *Shito Ryu Karate* that Sensei wrote. Years later, I believe around 1982 our Sensei Tamas Weber hosted Sensei Demura in his Dojo in Stockholm Sweden. I moved to the US in 1988 to direct action movies, and trained at Soke Tak Kubota's Dojo. At a reception for Japanese movie star Sonny Chiba, I noticed Demura Sensei but was too shy to talk to him. Kubota Sensei literally dragged me to Demura Sensei and introduced us. I mentioned that I was a student of Tamas Weber Sensei. Demura Sensei smiled and he said "Ah Tamas", and that's how we met.

Demura Sensei is the world's best ambassador of Karate. He travels and teaches anyone who asks him. His charm and mastery of skills of karate gave the art of Karate-do a tremendous amount of fame and respect world wide.

Chapter 9 – Growing the Organization

As I started having more presence in martial arts from my demonstrations, books, and exposure in the entertainment industry, I was also building more connections throughout the martial arts world. All of this effort had a powerful effect on my organization – at that time, the name of our organization was Itosu-Kai. I was receiving countless invitations to come do demonstrations and seminars from almost literally everywhere. Not only were students pouring into our Santa Ana dojo, but we were starting other California clubs and schools, and also bringing in students and schools joining us from all over the US and all over the world.

Our first school outside of California was started when one of my students, Bob Rose, moved to Joplin, Missouri to open a dojo in 1972. He opened a school on Main Street, just three doors down from a Goju-Ryu school run by a fellow named Lou Angel. Lou had a student who was a weapons star, and we spent many hours talking

Thoughts from Dave Jones

One of the earliest times Dave Jones, right, met Shihan.

I first met Shihan Demura in the mid 1970's in Joplin MO. At first, I was intimidated by his technique. But I was also grateful for his patience and willingness to share his technique and philosophy of training with us. Many Japanese instructors of the time appeared somewhat "distant" in their interactions with their students, but not Shihan Demura.

My real understanding of Shihan Demura began a couple of years later. Our original instructor, Mr. Bob Rose had decided to return to CA. The two of us that were the most senior were only 2nd or 3rd kyu at the time. We asked Shihan to keep the Dojo open and continue our studies with him. He agreed without hesitation.

The first time we brought him back to MO after Sensei Rose left, we were all concerned about making sure he was comfortable and had the best of everything. When I inquired how best to arrange his stay at a hotel, he said that he wanted to stay with me in my home. I replied that I had a small home with only one bedroom in it. His reply was "Do you have a couch I can sleep on?" I said, "Sensei it would not be proper for you to sleep on my couch!" But he insisted. For the week that he stayed with me he slept on my couch, and ate regular meals with me, refusing to be pampered. This is a trait that he carries on to this day. Showing that each person and their needs are important not just to them, but to the world around them. That no one doesn't deserve consideration, regardless of their status in life.

When I think back on the over 45 years of training under Demura Shihan, it is very hard to put into words what he has done for me. The heart of his instruction for me can best be described by the term "Chushin", which means "faithfulness", or "trueness". Demura Shihan has always been "faithful" to the heart of Budo instruction -- the helping of others. He has set for his students an example not only in the Dojo but in his life outside the Dojo that challenges each of us to develop the strength within ourselves not only to improve our Karate, but to improve our lives, and to help others find the strength within themselves to improve theirs. This is the heart of Budo and the legacy and challenge of Demura Shihan's instruction for me. I hope we all will continue to strive meet this challenge!!

about weapons. Unfortunately, Lou's school wasn't doing well, and he had to close it six months later.

Our Joplin school had a student named Dave Jones. I met Dave when I came out to the school to do a demonstration to get local people interested in the school, and have known him ever since. He is now one of our leading instructors and has been a wonderful friend all these years. He heads our school in North Carolina, and is a strong leader and contributor to the programs of all of our schools across the country, especially in our sword program.

When we were doing the Joplin demonstration, one spectator was a fellow from Kansas, named Dean Heinitz. He saw what we were doing and said "that's my karate" and immediately signed up and started training. Later on, Dean started our first Kansas school at the University of Pittsburg. Soon after, he rented a place and started a separate dojo on Broadway Street in Pittsburg, which has been there ever since. Later, Dean moved to Valley Center, Kansas and opened another school. One of Dean's students, Jim Otter, became the head instructor of the University and Broadway schools in Pittsburg.

Over the years, Jim has grown to become one of Genbu-Kai's strongest leaders.

Thoughts from Dean Heinitz

Dean Heinitz

Sensei came to my dojo in Valley Center, KS and would talk to the Black Belts about doing something besides just a tournament. I mentioned to him how we had done a tournament in the park on wet grass when I was studying with Sensei Bob Rose in Joplin, MO. At almost exactly the same time, Sensei and I both said that we could do a camp, and I told him I would set one up.

I set up the first camp at the local Salvation Army summer camp. We held the first camp in November of 1993. Sensei had such a good time and got to talk with and entertain our students with his stories that he spread the word to the other dojos around the world and camps sprang up all over the place. We will sponsor camp again in September 2018 marking 25 years since that first camp.

I could tell you more stories about Sensei's visit that year because that year was the first year we took him fishing in Missouri after the camp. At the camp there were two buildings for us to bunk down in. All of the girls were in one and all of the guys had the other. Sensei would snore so loud we all got to laughing and woke him up. There are so many wonderful stories about Sensei!

I remember when I decided I would drive all the way to Joplin, Missouri, all by myself to do a demonstration. I had a brand new white Toyota Camry. I owned that Camry for a lot of years, and as it got older some of my students said it absorbed so much of my personality that it was hard for anybody but me to drive it. Anyway, when it was brand new, I drove it by myself out to Joplin – and that was a very long, very unpleasant trip. I started getting sleepy, which scared me, so in the middle of the desert I stopped and slept underneath my car – very uncomfortable! Oh, and because it was a new car, I didn't have any license plates on it yet. Of course I got stopped by the police – twice. I never did that drive by myself ever again. In fact, that's when I started flying to our schools. I'd fly in to Joplin, Missouri, and then I'd fly over to Valley Center, Kansas – I started flying everywhere! After all these years I have flown so many places, and so many miles.

We not only did demonstrations for our own schools and events, but we received countless invitations to do demonstrations for other organizations and their events. Our new, exciting way of putting on our performances became enormously popular, bringing a lot of attention and appreciation and benefit to our group. I had a talented group of students that would go with me to do demonstrations, including Makoto Ibushi, Chuck Lanza, and Mike Anderson. These dedicated students helped me do spectacular demonstrations.

Thoughts from Jim Otter

Jim Otter

I started training in Demura Sensei's karate in August of 1977 while going to school at Pittsburg State University. Dean Heinitz was my first instructor. I first met Demura Sensei in the spring of 1978 at a seminar in Joplin, Missouri. He spent one evening at Pittsburg State for our rank testing. We were informed that very few people passed their tests under Demura Sensei so most of us where pretty sure we were going to fail. I was so impressed with Demura Sensei at this first meeting that I knew his karate was something I wanted to do. We were all impressed with his knowledge and skill in both karate and kobudo. To see him perform a kata was like living art in motion.

Since our first meeting, Demura Sensei has regularly traveled to Pittsburg, Kansas to guide our dojo's development with our seminars and tournaments. He became a close member of my entire family and two sons each were awarded their red belts and black belts, my wife her brown belt, and my daughter her blue belt (Sensei and my daughter also share their birthday). During our years together we have taken Sensei on many memorable fishing trips and trips to Branson, Missouri to see his friend, Mike Ito.

One of my favorite Demura experiences was traveling to Japan with him where we visited his home and family, and visited numerous historical sites that were important in his earlier life. He is a great tour guide and has a lot of knowledge, and I learned so much.

I was very honored that Demura Sensei was able to celebrate the Pittsburg Kansas dojo's 40th anniversary this year (2017). His annual visit to Pittsburg, Kansas always inspires our students to work harder and aspire to learn more about Demura karate.

It wasn't just demonstrations, though – these students also made big

impressions at all kinds of tournaments. At that time they were all

green belts, but we'd go to a tournament and I'd pick which one would go in each of the green belt, brown belt, and black belt sparring divisions, and they'd all win. By the way, before you ask, if a green belt fights in the black belt division, that's okay, because he's fighting people higher than his level – but you know you can't do it the other way around.

One time, we went to a Kenpo Karate Tournament in Tulsa, Oklahoma, and I put Makoto in the black belt division. Well, there was this one black belt who kept making hard contact on his opponents, even hitting them in the face – and then he'd grin every time he did it. Finally, he went up against Makoto, and Makoto wasn't going to put up with this guy's nonsense. Makoto came in hard with a front snap kick, and the guy lifted his knee, figuring that Makoto would hit his shin and hurt his foot, but instead Makoto's kick broke that guy's shin … and that guy wasn't smiling any more. Don't get me wrong – today we place safety above everything else in our tournaments – but there were definitely times and places when things were rougher, and I was pleased that my students could handle those situations very well.

Our organization grew again when one of my students, Don Zarlengo, moved to Winona, Minnesota and started teaching karate at the university there in 1972. He was doing okay, but started falling behind with keeping up his group, and he didn't communicate much with me. Luckily, one of his students, Fritz Speck, stepped up and took over the class. The first time I met Fritz, he came down to Kansas for one of our events. We talked for a long time, and I told him how he needed to reorganize the Minnesota group. He started doing a great job with leading that group, and it has gotten bigger and bigger ever since.

Thoughts from Bill Stoner

Sensei Demura and Bill Stoner, on the right, many years ago.

I have known Sensei Demura since 1975, and I consider him one of my very closest friends. I met him in Vegas, where he let me be part of his show. We have traveled everywhere together, and he has taught me so much about karate and about how to teach karate, especially to children. My heart is full of the memories, the fun ones and the serious ones, of everything we have shared.

We moved into Pennsylvania and New York, too. Bill Stoner was already training with the Kyokushinkai group in Pittsburgh. He happened to be in Las Vegas in 1975 and saw our act. Right away,

he made a point of coming out to California to see me and join our

group. Bill has been a tough, powerful supporter and great friend

since we met.

Thoughts from Charles Hobbib

Charles Hobbib

When I first started training, I would read about Sensei Demura in magazines, and it was my dream to meet him. After many years of training I got up the courage to call him, and to eventually plan a trip to California to meet him in 1981. When I got to his dojo, the first words he said to me were "I hope you didn't come here to receive another black belt, because you won't get one! I replied, "No Sensei, I just came to train with a great Master!" and he smiled. He showed me the dressing room and told me to sleep there. I slept on an old couch with hole in the cushions. Every year after that I would come out for two weeks for at least 80 hours of training. When he told me I was to be his east coast representative, I couldn't have been prouder! Thank you for everything, Master Demura!

Right around 1980, Charles Hobbib, who was part of Hayashi-Ha in

New York, saw me in *Black Belt Magazine*, and called me to ask if

he could come to California to join our group. At the time Charles

came to California for the first time, Makoto, who was by then a

black belt, was living in the dojo. Makoto was running late for class,

so he grabbed a white belt from the shelf to wear to class. During class I told people to pair up for kumite (sparring). I remember Charles picked Makoto because he thought he was a white belt. Charles was having fun, and was coming pretty hard at Makoto, and the next thing I knew, Charles was flying out the back door! He came running back in and asked Makoto "Are you sure you're a white belt?" Makoto just said "Don't ask." I loved it – people shouldn't assume they know what someone else can do, and definitely don't try to run over somebody – that person just might surprise you – I know Charles sure was surprised!

Thoughts from Mark Martinez

Mark Martinez, left, and Sensei Demura

Hajime!
My Eucalyptus Sensei
Your roots run wide and deep,
and both can break through concrete.
Your feet stand firm onto the ground,
like the stump that doesn't bend.
When a branch breaks, multiple
branches grow and take its place.
Your passion for karate burns hot and long.
Your leaves are like our Kiai and Seiza,
both help our lungs and give us mental clarity.
Yame!
Gracias, Sensei

Itosu-Kai just kept getting bigger and bigger all over the United States. Then we started going international. Around 1980 one of our instructors, Mark Martinez, started taking groups of our students down to events in Mexico, and started getting to know the instructors who were teaching in several locations there. In 1986, one of these instructors, Fernando Duron, along with one of his students, Rojelio Ayala, asked about joining my group, and ever since then we have added many more schools and students to our Mexico group.

Our other earliest international direction was to Canada. There was a guy in Canada named Cam Steuart who had been reading about me in magazines for many years, and drove down to meet me. He had earned a Shotokan black belt from the Japan Karate Association, but didn't have a school of his own. At that time, we were still in the process of transitioning from the Shotokan style to Shito-Ryu. Cam joined Itosu-Kai, and started our first classes in Canada. Cam has a great head for organization, and he has built a very large presence for our group in Canada, and the biggest group in Genbu-Kai. Cam is a strong, demanding, highly effective leader, and he and his students contribute enormously to our organization.

Thoughts from Cam Steuart

Cam Steuart

I first became aware of Demura Sensei in the late 1960's when he appeared in an issue of Black Belt magazine. He was demonstrating the use of the Sai which I found to be very intriguing. Over the next few years he would, from time to time, be featured in that magazine and I would read the article with great interest and dream about the possibility of meeting and training with him. Sometime later I happened to travel to California and found my way to his dojo on Bristol Street in Santa Ana. The dojo was a beehive of activity, with class in full session and Demura Sensei there in middle directing the training in his dynamic and vigorous way. I stood in the doorway and watched, as I'm sure many such visitors did, and was in awe of the energy and atmosphere which existed in that small building. Several years would pass before I would stand in that doorway again and this time it was to inquire about joining his organization. I had just returned from two years in Japan teaching English and practicing karate and Iaido. I had started a club in a small Canadian city and wanted to affiliate with a larger group. Over the years, I had always remembered that visit to Demura Sensei's dojo and that was exactly what I wanted for my fledgling group of students. Nearly thirty-three years have passed since that day and the excitement and the gratification of being one of Sensei's students has not abated in the least. Over the many years, thousands of members from our group of dojos in Canada have benefitted from being a part of his organization and from being able to train and simply spend time with Sensei. He has truly touched the hearts and minds of all those who have been a part of the journey.

As we were growing our organization, sometimes unfortunate things happened. A guy from Pakistan, Javitz Akram, contacted me and asked if he could come to visit our Santa Ana dojo, so I sent him an invitation so he could get a visa. When he left, he was supposed to go back to Pakistan, but I found out later that he didn't – he went to New York and became a cab driver, but he wasn't legal. I require our people to be honorable, and it has always bothered me that Javitz behaved the way he did. Even so, I felt very bad when I heard that a few years ago he was murdered.

Sometimes we would move into new countries in interesting ways. For example, we had a school in Venezuela, headed by Ling Sung Mock. This group joined with us after I met Ling Sung while doing a demonstration in Guatemala. Ling Sung had been a part of the Shito-Kai organization, but joined my Itosu-Kai group after meeting me, and there we were with a school in Venezuela. Ling Sung had a student of his own, who was a young man from Greece, Bassilio Bessis. After receiving his Black Belt, Bassilio, returned to his home country of Greece, and he started our first school in Greece.

The same kind of thing happened in other parts of Europe. One of my students from when I taught in Japan was a man named Kitamura. He had a student of his own, Mieno, who went to Spain to open a school in Malaga. Some years later I was conducting a seminar in Spain, and Mieno realized who I was and our connection, and made an effort to come and introduce himself. His school joined our group, and that was our first school in Spain. And speaking of Spain, we also went there by way of opening our first school in Germany. A fellow named Roman Westfehling in Germany read about me in a magazine, and came to California to train with me. After that he went back to Germany and opened our first German school. Years later he moved to Spain to make more schools there.

Thoughts from Roman Westfehling

Roman Westfehling, left, and Fumio Demura
in Lübeck, Germany, 1991.

I had trained for many years in Shotokan before I came to know Sensei Demura. In Germany, we didn't have much good information about karate and kobudo, but I kept looking. Finally I found Sensei's books on karate and all of the weapons he taught, and it was wonderful. I knew, though, that nothing was as good as instruction in class. One time, a visiting Master, Al Dacascos, came to teach, and I found out he was friends with Sensei Demura. I started communicating with him, and in 1981 he let me come to stay in his dojo and go to every class I could – even children's classes. I learned so much and was able to bring it back to Germany. Finally, after many years of training, I was able to test for my Shito-Ryu Black Belt with Sensei Demura, and officially start representing him in Europe. Being his student has been fulfilling in every way.

Our Chilean group was created in a very different way. For a long time, the leader of Chile, Augusto Pinochet, had strict rules regarding the teaching of martial arts in Chile, so we did not have a school there. However, Mr. Pinochet had heard of me and asked me to come to Chile and do a demonstration for him, and I brought Chuck Lanza with me. We held a seminar in front of Mr. Pinochet, and I was able meet some of the karate students in Chile. We also had a very exciting experience when one of their most famous talk show hosts, Don Francisco (he was the Johnny Carson of Chile), had us appear on his TV show for an interview and to show a few techniques. Some years later, when Mr. Pinochet was no longer the leader of Chile, a young brown belt named Fernando Soto, who knew of me from his prior instructor, contacted me hoping to become my student. Since that time, Fernando has worked hard to expand his expertise, and now he does a good job of running our large group of schools in Chile.

Thoughts from Doug Stein

Doug Stein

I first met Sensei in the fall of 1996. I train in Shotokan, but I had heard that Sensei Demura had a Rengo-Kai arm in his organization, and I was very interested in joining. A mutual friend arranged for us to meet in Miami International Airport when Sensei had a lay-over on his way to South America (this was in the old days when people freely came and went in airports). Soon, my Florida school was part of his organization.

Sensei is one of the greatest instructors ever. One time he showed me that in a very unexpected way. He and I were sitting at a table watching a competition. Suddenly he said to me "you don't practice your karate." I was confused, and started stammering out lame excuses. In the middle of my stammering, Sensei just turns his head to me with that kindly menacing look, and tells me to shut up. He then raises an eyebrow as he shifts his eyes towards his own shoulder and ever so slightly pulls his shoulders back. It struck me harder than a zuki to the jaw. Sensei was telling me that I was slumping in my seat and that reflected a lack of discipline and self-respect - characteristics inherent to the study of karate. Indeed, I was not practicing my karate. It was the greatest karate lesson I ever had. Karate is not just what takes place in the dojo while in a gi. Rather, karate teaches principles that should become part of your everyday living. Thank you, Sensei. I never have, and never will forget that most important lesson.

Over the years, our group has grown by creating relationships and adding schools in a great many countries, including Panama, South Africa, France, Poland, New Zealand, England, Australia, India, and many others. Our most successful foreign schools are our groups in

Canada and Chile, and this is because they follow all of my methods of teaching and organizing.

In the US, we are always growing, and now have schools in New Jersey, Michigan, Arizona, Indiana, Georgia, Florida, Colorado, Virginia, Ohio, and adding more all the time. Some of our dojos in other states join our organization, but continue to practice another style, like Shotokan, and those schools are part of our Rengo-Kai program. One of our instructors in Florida, Doug Stein, has been a strong leader in the Rengo-Kai part of our organization.

My California schools are always growing and changing, and, as I mentioned before, the Santa Ana Dojo is where I keep my office and conduct the business of our organization. We are working on the new building we moved into this year (2017), and, although it will never replace our beloved old Santa Ana Dojo, it is turning into a fine new home for our organization's headquarters – our new Honbu Dojo.

Chapter 10 – Traveling

My students know me for being a big traveler in the US and all over the world. I try to visit all of our Genbu-Kai schools at least once per year, although that's not always easy, these days. I also used to spend a lot more time traveling to other organizations' events, doing seminars and demonstrations, and there are still many special outside groups and events that we participate in today. Also, I will travel to meet with new groups that want to become part of my organization. However, although I enjoy both going to new places and visiting our many schools, traveling is not always a pleasant experience.

Many years ago I traveled to Costa Rica for the first time to meet with an instructor who wanted to have his school join our group. I stayed in the man's home, and he was very hospitable, but it wasn't too fun to find out that the shower was a gallon can with the hose from the yard coming in the top of it and holes punched for the water to come out the bottom. Later in the visit, I did go to a hotel, and the thing that really bothered me most was when he asked one of his students to take me to my hotel, and the guys said "Why don't you do it yourself?" I could see that he wasn't as strong an instructor as he should be – he didn't teach good values to his students. We kept working, though, and now our Costa Rica group is headed by Alberto Paris, a dedicated instructor who does a very good job.

Thoughts from Stavros Costarangos

From the left Lionel Worrell (Panama); Cameron Steuart (Canada); Wingfong Mock (Venezuela); Osvaldo Diaz (Panama); Shihan Fumio Demura; Yoji Sakamoto (Honduras); David Hines (USA) – at Karate Kamp 1996 Panama at El Valle de Anton

I first met Sensei when he came to Panama. He asked us about our accomplishments, and we tried to impress him with our many kumite awards. That was the wrong approach! He said "Show me kata" and we came to understand that he is unique. His view is to the long term, not to flashy accomplishments, and he shows us this constantly in the dojo and in life. Anecdotes and accomplishments by Demura Sensei, carry an imbedded teaching for all of us as his students. Not only in the dojo with his sharing of his immense karate and budo knowledge, but outside of dojo in his approach to everyday life, that has had him confront adversity, ups and downs, laughter and tears, with a self-imposed responsibility to be a leader, an instructor, and an example to follow. He did not seek conformity with the way of the empty hand alone, but also continues to hand down to us and the world his Kobudo, Batto-Do, Taiko, Iai-Do, Kendo, Shuji, Origami, and more to follow. Our Genbu-Kai Budo Family is what we will cherish as a legacy that Demura Sensei has given to us in life.

Another time, an instructor from Panama, Osvaldo Diaz, wanted to bring his group into mine. He came to California to meet with me, and then I went to Panama to see his school. At that time, Manuel Noriega was the leader of Panama. It was common practice for visitors like me to have a bodyguard, and Osvaldo had arranged for an off-duty policeman to be my bodyguard – and that turned out to be a very good thing. One day I was having a meal in a restaurant with Osvaldo and one of his students, and I was asking about Noriega and what was going on in their country.

Next thing, I felt a gun touch the back of my head.

Luckily, Noriega's man listened when my bodyguard told him I was not being disrespectful and did not mean anything bad about what I was saying. Later when we went back to my hotel, my bodyguard told me he should come with me. When we got to my room, we saw the door was half open, and that my room had been searched. He went in first to see if it was safe, and nobody was there, and nothing was missing. They must have known who I was and where I was staying even before Noriega's man aimed his gun at me. Right after

I left Panama, the US invaded, and the war started. Today, of course, Panama is a very pleasant place to visit, and we have a good school there headed by Stavros Costarangos, a dedicated instructor and good friend.

Another frightening trip was to Guatemala – I went by myself, but met a man there who had read about me in a magazine, and we became friends. He was in the CIA! He knew something was going to happen, and he told me to leave right away. I flew out immediately, and it ended up being right before the airport was closed because of revolution.

Another difficult trip was when I went to the Dominican Republic. I went with Ling Sung Mock, who at that time was the head of our Venezuela group. One thing I always did when going to a new country was to visit the US embassy that was close to where I was visiting, and that ended up being a very good thing on this trip. We had finished our teaching we were doing for the day, and I went to the embassy to say hello. Right away, the man who met with me said I should get on a plane and leave the country, and the next day I went to the airport. To my surprise, the man from the embassy was there with his wife, daughter, and son, and he asked me to take them with me on the plane. The next day war started. Unfortunately, Ling Sung was not able to leave at the same time, and he stayed in his hotel, literally hearing bullets go by. It was another week before he could return to Venezuela.

Not every scary trip involves bullets, and not every scary trip was a long time ago. About three years ago I was in Chile when a big earthquake hit. Fernando Soto, the head of our Chilean group, had a condominium on the 34th floor, and that's where I was when everything started shaking. Now I've been in many earthquakes, but nothing like that one. I literally believed that the building would fall down, it was shaking so badly – and things would have ended up very bad with falling from the 34th floor. I have rarely been so thoroughly scared.

One of the worst trips was when 911 happened. I was getting ready to go home from visiting Dean Heinitz' school in Kansas, and Bill Stoner was with me in a hotel room that we were sharing in Branson,

Missouri. I had the TV on and was watching CNN. I remember

thinking that what I was watching had to be a movie or TV show,

and I asked Bill if CNN showed movies. It just didn't seem real that

an airplane had hit the World Trade Center. We watched, and then

saw the second crash, and we knew that it was all very, very real. I

called Dean, and then I called the airport – of course it was closed.

Bill and I went to stay at Dean's house, and it seemed like we would

never get to go home. I wanted to drive to Texas, or maybe even all

the way to California, but nobody wanted me to do that. After three

days I'd finally had enough, and I went to the airport to wait for a

seat on a plane. I was able to get on a plane, and took flights from

Kansas to Dallas, Texas; then Dallas to San Francisco, California;

then San Francisco to Seattle, Washington; and finally from Seattle

to Orange County, California.

Coincidentally, right after I got back from that trip, we had already

planned a fishing trip to Mexico with a few of my students,

including Kevin Suzuki, Thanh Nguyen, and Frank Almeida.

Charles Hobbib from New York was supposed to come for that trip,

but you can probably guess that right after 911 a person with the last name Hobbib would have problems traveling, so he didn't come. We got on a boat in San Diego and boated down to the Mexican coast to fish. On our way back north to the US, all the boats in the area, about 50, or so, were lined up by government officials and they checked all of our IDs. It was probably a really good idea that Charles didn't come on that trip.

On a different fishing trip to San Lucas, Mexico, the danger was the weather. This particular trip was a gift from my students for my 40th anniversary teaching in the US, which we celebrated in 2005. I went on this trip with a couple of my students, including Dwight Lomayesva (I mentioned him earlier) and another guy named Damon Pace, who now heads our Colorado school. We were out on a fishing boat and a terrible storm came up. What made it even scarier was that we had to jump from the fishing boat onto a small boat so that we could get to the shore. The waves were more than ten feet high, and it was absolutely terrifying to try to time those jumps as the boats bounced up and down in those waves. We were all very, very lucky that nobody was hurt, and we made it home safely.

I've also been to the Middle East, and that was another kind of scary altogether. Back in 1979, I was invited by Aramco, an oil company in Saudi Arabia, to participate in a kind of executives retreat. They had all sorts of special activities with celebrities for the managers of their company, like a UCLA basketball star teaching them basketball, and a martial arts film star (me, from *Island of Dr. Moreau*) teaching them karate. One of my students, Dave Javier, came with me to assist me – coincidentally, he was in a Chuck Norris movie called *Breaker, Breaker*, and our hosts liked that.

Teaching executives wasn't the scary part. When we got off the plane, government officials took our passports away and gave us a list of rules we had to follow, or we'd be put in jail. We couldn't look at women, we couldn't drink any alcohol – luckily the rules were not hard to follow, but still it's not fun knowing how easy it could be to end up in serious trouble. On top of that, when we would drive through the desert from place to place, we'd see things like dead camels that had their stomachs exploded from the heat, and cars that had been in crashes and then just left on the side of the road.

Some things would start off a bit scary, but then end up being very surprising. One time we flew in a little plane with two propellers going to a town farther away, and there were chickens and a cow on that flight with us. And another time when an American guy invited us out to a restaurant, we drove for a long time way out to the middle of the desert and when we got there all we could see at first was a building with a single light bulb. It looked kind of bad on the outside of the building, but inside it was a paradise like in a movie, and everything was very rich and lavish with a big fountain in the middle. In general, though, water was scarce, so people didn't shower as often as we were used to, and you can imagine it was hard to get used to that. As a souvenir they gave me an outfit of traditional Arab clothing. Although I've never worn it, I do still have it, as well as the vivid memories of that trip.

A few years ago, I visited the Middle East again, this time on a trip to Qatar. It was different than that long ago visit to Saudi Arabia.

This time I was there to teach university karate students. I also got to visit a Japanese elementary school, and I taught the children some origami, which is one of my very favorite things to do when I am relaxing. On this trip, though, the scary part happened a week after I came home – the town where I had taught Japanese children how to do origami had been bombed and totally destroyed. I know I am very lucky that I was already gone by the time that town was bombed, and I hope very, very much that the children, and the other people I met while I was in Qatar, were not hurt.

Chapter 11 – Kobudo and Batto-Do

As you already know, I have a deep interest in the development of Kobudo and Batto-Do. I have explored many ways to expand these disciplines and also make them more accessible to the American public, and to the world.

When I first came to the US, I found the kobudo scene a bit baffling. There were many schools and students, but not much structure or consistency. When I would judge at tournaments, the variety of weapons seemed rather arbitrary, and it seemed like many of the katas were home-made. The judges were not very capable, but how could they be if there was no real structure to the discipline? I had come from a very structured and consistent kobudo environment, filled with tradition and depth of expertise. It became very apparent to me that a lot of work was needed.

As I mentioned earlier, I started demonstrating weapons at tournaments, one of the first being my sai demonstration at Ed

Parker's tournament in Long Beach, California. Then I started teaching my students about kobudo. I also started writing books, as I mentioned earlier, which continue to be popular today.

In my own organization, I began working on the structure of kobudo training. First I narrowed the number of weapons I taught to a selection of traditional Okinawan weapons – nunchaku, sai, tonfa, kama, bo, and eku-bo. Then I started teaching the traditional katas from my training in Japan. Those traditional kobudo katas, though, were long, intricate, and difficult to master. This made students reluctant to take on training in kobudo, which limited the possibilities for expanding student interest. I decided to create a series of basic (kihon) katas – at least one for each weapon – which were shorter and easier to learn, and easier and more consistent to judge in competition. Then I started holding seminars in various weapons for my own organization, and for other organizations, as well, which included the basic katas I had developed and different attack and defense techniques. My seminars also often included a simple competition so that students could immediately display their new skills, which gave them a lot of encouragement to train further.

I focused a great deal on training some of my junior students in kobudo. One student, Kevin Suzuki, started training in karate as a very little boy. He had enormous interest and ability, and started training in kobudo in addition to karate. Kevin is one of our highly respected instructors in both arts, and has been a great resource as I have expanded our seminar and competition program for kobudo.

Thoughts from Kevin Suzuki

Sensei Demura with Kevin Suzuki

I have known Sensei for just about my whole life, and I have many wonderful memories of being in the junior class when he was teaching. My favorite activity with Sensei was the Sumo Challenge. All the students would line up around the back and side walls. One at a time Sensei would play Sumo with each of us. At the end, Sensei would select a couple of us to team up against him. Sensei would say "If you guys lose, it will be one hundred push-ups". My sister and I were sometimes selected. We would hold on the Sensei's legs and not let go. We struggled, pulled, pushed, and used all our might to beat Sensei. In the end we always had push-ups. All these activities Sensei did in class were so much fun. All the kids loved it and I know Sensei enjoyed making all the sounds effects, grunts, yells and facial expressions to scare some kids or encourage others. This was Sensei's fun time and he smiled a lot.

Over the years, I have also incorporated some highly specialized katas in kobudo training, competitions, and demonstrations. We have had students become extremely capable at some of these more esoteric katas. For example, we had students become very proficient at the double-nunchaku – this is where there is a nunchaku in each hand, often being swung at the same time, which makes for a very dramatic demonstration.

Thoughts from Thanh Nguyen

On the set of the movie Ninja – from the left, Ken Nishiki, Elisa Au, Fumio Demura, Thanh Nguyen, Danny Kim, and Thomas Shinoda. The four men with Sensei Demura are his students.

I have known Sensei Demura for most of my life. He has taught me countless techniques and katas in karate and kobudo, and I have been very fortunate to have the gift of being able to perform them well and help teach them to my fellow Genbu-Kai students. Also, as part of Sensei's team, I have traveled to many, many places with him and performed demonstrations and led seminars, helping him in the effort to share his expertise. I am very proud and happy to be a part of what Sensei Demura has built from his inspiration and never-ending energy and hard work.

Thanh Nguyen, who is now one of our most highly regarded instructors in both karate and kobudo, became an expert in furi-kama. Furi-kama incorporates both kama being rapidly swung and twirled from cords around the wrists. At first, Thanh sometimes would do the furi-kama demonstration with a live (sharp) kama in each hand, but one time he gave himself a very bad cut on the arm, which fortunately ended up being a very lucky lesson for all of our students, instead of the tragedy it could have been. One of our other students, Jacki Long, who is also one of our most highly appreciated karate instructors, used to compete with live kama, until one time she cut off her pony tail in competition, which was a very frightening experience for everyone who saw it happen!

Thoughts from Jacki Long

From left David Hines, Carlos Cuero, Sensei Demura,
Jacki Long, and Dwight Lomayesva – 1979.

I have a lot of stories from the 46 years I've known Demura Sensei, but this is one that shows his sense of humor. It was after day class in the old honbu dojo, maybe 1977. I was a brown belt and practicing after class alone on the tatami. John Roper came in and said "Sensei wants to see you." I went to the office immediately. Demura sensei said "I want you to break this board." Doug Ivan, Makoto Ibushi, Chuck Lanza, Dan Kerr, Carlos Cuero, Mr. Ivan, and John Roper were all sitting there. I had never broken a board or even considered it. John said he would hold it for me, and I think I heard some snickering. I do remember thinking to myself that Sensei wouldn't ask me if he didn't think I could do it. Why I chose to use a shuto (knifehand strike), I will never know, but luckily it worked, and the board snapped in half! Then Demura Sensei said, "Oh good, we didn't know if the wood was dry yet."

We have been very fortunate that such lessons were not as disastrous as they could have been, and since then I have demanded that my students train and perform safely.

With kobudo kata development well under way, I then turned my attention to kobudo kumite (sparring with weapons). In the 90's I started with my first attempts to have my students spar with weapons. Of course there were obvious safety issues. Even weapons made with less dangerous materials than wood and metal were still very dangerous. I brought over expensive Kendo armor equipment from Japan to protect people when sparring. It did protect the students, but unfortunately it was also very difficult to put on and take off – students needed one or even two people to help them, and it took a lot of time. Then, with all of the equipment on, students couldn't see or hear clearly, and needed to be shouted at and led into position so they could spar. There were fun experiences – when our group would hold small competitions the armor gave many opportunities for humor – but it would never be an effective way to develop sparring with weapons.

Then I had a breakthrough – in the early 2000's I met an inventive fellow named Dana Abbott, and together we designed and produced sparring weapons with a brand new approach that all but eliminated the danger. Students no longer needed to wear clunky armor – they could do very well with just a lightweight helmet and a pair of sparring gloves. We were able to enormously reduce the expense, time, and effort involved with kobudo kumite training and competitions. The most important part, though, was the positively revolutionary benefits for students! Without the old armor, and thanks to the wonderfully improved weapons, students could move freely and much more quickly. They also had the freedom to focus on developing and applying technique without unnecessary anxiety about hurting their opponent. Of course we still always focus on safety – that must never be neglected.

Suddenly training in weapons sparring was available to everyone – all ages and levels of experience could jump in and have fun. We used it at every kobudo seminar, and as I'm sure you guessed, if you didn't already know, it was an amazing hit! Right away we started developing effective ways to add it to our competitions, and now it is a standard part of many kobudo tournaments all over the country.

Over the last few years I have also implemented a highly effective testing and ranking system that incorporates all of our developments in kobudo training and instruction. Student are inspired to become proficient in kobudo training. We will continue developing kobudo and making it available to as many students as we can.

Separate from our other weapons training, we also have sword training. As I mentioned earlier, I studied Iai-Do in Japan and early on I started training some of my American students in that discipline. In those early years, our sword program was very small, and sword students could only compete in our regular weapons competitions in divisions with other weapons. Of course, the elegance of sword kata did not have the raw energy and excitement of other weapons, but at that time we did not have enough interest in sword training for tournaments. Since then we have developed separate sword tournaments so students can enjoy competing in this elegant art.

You might recall that earlier I mentioned that I had trained with Taizaburo Nakamura in Kendo, and that he later went to become an internationally recognized Master of Batto-Do. Perhaps you also recall that I mentioned that Minoru Nishiki, the brother of my best friend Isamu, was important to our sword program. Well, Minoru had started training with Mr. Nakamura in Batto-Do in Japan. In 1989, in yet another wonderful combination of relationships, Minoru brought together Mr. Nakamura and myself. Mr. Nakamura came to America, and he and I started my Batto-Do program. We started doing demonstrations and increasing training opportunities, and our students developed a great deal of interest in the sword. Before he passed away in 2003, Mr. Nakamura told me he wanted to spread Batto-Do throughout the world, and I vowed to him that it would be my mission to make his dream a reality.

Taizaburo Nakamura, left, on one of his visits to my school.

In our early Batto-Do years, we focused mostly on the eight established Toyama-Ryu katas. We started bringing over other Japanese Batto-Do and Iai-Do Masters, such as Seiji Ueki, Takeshi Mochizuki, Kazuhiko Hosaka, and other Masters, who also helped my students extensively with these katas. Over the years, these Masters would come and train my students and also do amazing cutting demonstrations at our international tournament, which audiences enjoyed very much. Unfortunately some of those cherished Masters have passed on, and in more recent years, Mr. Choji Sato has been our most frequent annual visitor.

We also added cutting to our training. It can be very difficult and very expensive to get real Japanese swords. In those early years we used stainless steel swords – many American knife shops sell sword sets designed to look like authentic Japanese swords – which we would spend many hours sharpening. However, I found a fellow named Paul Chen who had developed a process of making swords that was very close to the traditional methods used by Masters in Japan. I was able to help my students buy very good swords from him, which added a new level of elegance to our program. These newer swords were also much better for training in cutting technique.

Over time, I realized that the sword program needed the same kind of fundamental development that I had made with my kobudo program. I developed eight basic sword katas, that I call Kome Katas. They are based on the eight directions of cutting. Kome, which means rice, is a character of kanji that actually shows the eight angles of cutting.

You may not know that Batto katas are usually performed from a standing position, and Iai katas are generally performed from a kneeling position. As you might guess, the Iai katas can be difficult to perform if the student has a knee problem, and martial arts students frequently develop knee problems over a long period of time. It occurred to me that it would be a good idea to create a series of advanced Batto katas that would be based on Iai katas, but performed from a standing position. These new katas, which I have been developing for the past few years, allow sword students to continue to advance their training and also allow them to benefit from the influences of both Batto and Iai. I call these katas Suishin-Ryu, which means water heart.

I chose this name because water has so many wonderful characteristics that I find useful when teaching my students. First, we need water for life, along with almost every living thing in our world – in other words, it is essential to our being. Also, water can deal with any situation with no harm to itself. It moves easily out of the way when touched. It easily fills any shape of container it goes into. Water can find the smallest opening to get around or through any obstacle. It can move any obstacle, sometimes slowly over time, and sometimes with ferocious speed, but ultimately the power of water is irresistible.

With my Batto-Do program, as with my kobudo program, I have also created a highly effective testing and ranking system that incorporates all of our developments in sword training and instruction. We will continue developing our Batto-Do program and making it available to as many students as we can.

Thoughts from Choji Sato

Sword Master from Japan Choji Sato

I am delighted that Sensei Demura is writing his autobiography. He has been teaching and producing excellent karate students for over 50 years in the United States. He is an excellent martial artist, an excellent leader, and an excellent teacher.

In the dojo, he has many children as his students. He teaches them not only physical aspects of martial arts but also guides them to live as good human beings, and always to have a thankful heart. There are many people who went on to have successful careers and other life ventures after receiving guidance from Sensei Demura. I personally do not do karate, but I have learned a lot from Sensei Demura through his life stories and his teachings on how one should associate with people.

Sensei Demura has many accomplishments, but the one that impresses me the most is that he has created a whole new Batto-Do organization, Suishin Itto-Ryu Batto-Do, and he has also developed whole new sets of katas to broaden and enhance the art of Batto-Do. This could only have been achieved by a person with the deep understanding of swordsmanship that Demura Sensei has developed.

I look forward to Sensei Demura's continued success in teaching traditional martial arts to more and more people and spreading the true value of traditional martial arts to the world.

Chapter 12 – Itosu-Kai and Genbu-Kai

Some of you who have known me for a long time know that for many years our organization was called Itosu-Kai. This is because Itosu-Kai was Mr. Sakagami's organization. Mr. Sakagami was my Sensei, and so of course I was part of his organization, and when I came to America, I was the head of the American arm of Itosu-Kai. In Japan, organizations such as Itosu-Kai are generally passed from generation to generation within families, so when Mr. Sakagami died in 1994, his son Sadaki inherited the responsibility for heading the organization. This presented difficulties for the new head of Itosu-Kai, because many of Mr. Sakagami's students, myself included, were of higher rank than Sadaki was.

A few years later, I was taken ill and needed double-bypass open heart surgery. At that time, unbeknownst to me, one of my students went to Japan and tried to have himself made the head of the American Itosu-Kai group in my place. The next thing I knew, there was a harsh letter going out to the members of Itosu-Kai filled with untrue statements about me, and declaring that I was no longer part of Itosu-Kai. I was truly horrified and sickened that one of my students had made this happen. I was saddened, but unsurprised, that Japan Itosu-Kai was willing to take this step.

The next day I "got up after falling down" and created my own group, Shito-Ryu Karate-Do Genbu-Kai. To my great pleasure and satisfaction, almost every one of my schools stayed with me and officially joined my new group. My original Venezuelan group decided to stay with Itosu-Kai, but a couple of years later, Edgar Albakian, one of the students from the earlier group, formed his own school and "re-"joined my Genbu-Kai organization.

I chose the name Genbu-Kai for a specific reason. I have always been inspired by and admired the history of the Genbu-Kan, which was a kind of academy in Japan where many prominent leaders and historical figures studied the ways of the samurai. This school was founded by Chusaku Chiba in Japan's Edo Era. Chusaku Chiba, a very famous sword Master and Japanese historical figure, was noted for innovative thought and training. For example, the kendo training in the Genbu-Kan went from using a bokken (a solid piece of wood shaped like a sword) to using a shinai (a lightweight instrument constructed of flexible pieces of bamboo). This change was revolutionary in creating safer, more effective training for kendo students.

Many leaders and prominent members of society trained at the Genbu-Kan. One of the most famous students, Ryoma Sakamoto, was famous for urging modern change in Japanese society. In the Edo Era, Japan was ruled by Shogun. Ryoma Sakamoto wanted to bring a new form of leadership to Japan. Although he was assassinated in 1867, his work to change Japan was successful. In 1867 the Edo Era ended, and in 1868 the Meiji Era began. Swords were no longer carried, and people started wearing western clothing and hairstyles. This was the beginning of Emperor rule in Japan. At that same time, there was another Genbu-Kan student, Hirobumi Ito, who was also very influential in Japanese society and politics. He helped implement many political changes and eventually rose to become the first Prime Minister of Japan.

By the way, in 1961, when I won the first All-Japan Kumite Champion, one of my trophies was handed to me by the Prime Minister at that time, Hayato Ikeda – it was a very great honor.

For its great impact on the development of Japan, I admired the history of Genbu-Kan, and the fact that so many important and influential people trained there. It was a clear choice to me that our new organization should reflect, and hopefully continue, that great legacy of being a positive and effective influence on people, culture, and society.

Chapter 13 – Now and the Future

There is one topic I have declined to address in this book, although I'm sure there has always been much curiosity about it, and perhaps people expected me to include it. That is the subject of romance. It is my personal decision, as it always has been, that this is not something I will discuss, except to silently acknowledge here those special people who have touched my life in that way. For better or worse, I always have been and always will be "married" to karate.

As many of you know, in recent years I have faced some pretty serious health problems. In 2011, I suffered a subdural hematoma (bleeding in my head). In emergency surgery, the doctor removed the blood, but said I only had a 5% chance of surviving, and I was in a coma for several days. Much to the doctor's surprise, though, within a few weeks I was in physical therapy and starting to eat solid food. I was delighted as I started being able to again do more and more of the things that are important to me. This experience also gave me numerous opportunities to touch even more lives, in many unexpected ways, and I can honestly say I am grateful for those opportunities.

It was a very interesting experience when producers started filming a documentary about my life, called *The Real Miyagi*. They had started the filming a bit before my 45th Anniversary Teaching in the United States, which occurred in 2010. Production was still going on when I fell ill in 2011, and continued while I was recovering. The first screening was in 2015, just in time for my 50th Anniversary Teaching in the United States. 2015 was an extraordinary year.

A couple of years ago, my kidneys stopped functioning. The doctor put me on dialysis and a special diet. Surprisingly, I have regained considerable kidney function, although I still need dialysis. I have adapted to my health requirements, and am able to perform my dialysis at home and even on trips. I may not travel quite as much as I did before, but I still manage to go many places, both in the US and abroad. Throughout all of my health issues, my family and students have been constantly by my side, providing support and assistance.

I continue to teach students in the dojo and in seminars far and wide, and I continue to build and further develop our organization and the arts we practice. Daily I talk to people I know and people new to me. I am often asked to participate in new activities and events. I have new ideas and directions I want to pursue, including writing more books and creating more videos. As we wrap up the writing of this book, we are busily planning events large and small for the next two years, and longer. In quiet relaxation, I create origami cranes, which I give to those around me in moments that delight me as much as they do the people who receive the cranes.

What does the future hold? For as long as I am able, I will keep moving forward. That is all any of us can do, and I am pleased and grateful that I can continue to contribute to the lives of the people around me.

Thank you for reading my story. I hope you found it interesting. I hope you enjoyed reading it as much as I enjoyed writing it. Arigatou gozaimashita.

Appendix: Kobudo Weapons

It occurs to me that some people reading this book may not know what the weapons are that I talk about. Here are pictures and names of the weapons, so you can see what my students have studied.

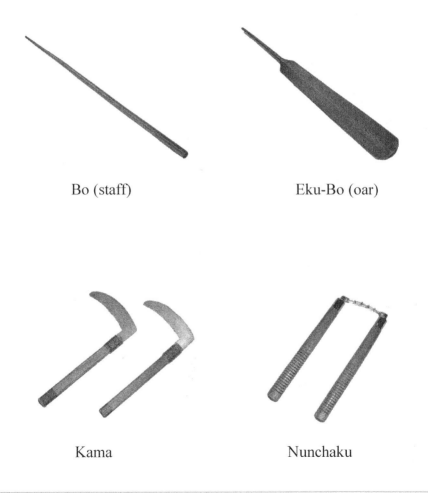

Bo (staff)   Eku-Bo (oar)

Kama   Nunchaku

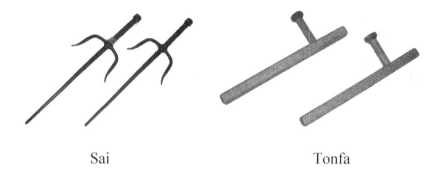

Sai   Tonfa

Appendix: Genbu-Kai Schools

At the time this book is being written,
we have schools in these places.

United States

Arizona
California
Colorado
Connecticut
Florida
Georgia
Indiana
Kansas
Michigan
Minnesota
Missouri
New Jersey
New York
North Carolina
Ohio
Pennsylvania
West Virginia

Other Countries

Argentina
Australia
Canada
Chile
Costa Rica
England
France
Germany
Greece
Honduras
India
Japan
Mexico
New Zealand
Panama
Poland
Qatar
South Africa
Spain
Venezuela

Appendix: Fumio Demura's History

Mr. Demura has received recognition and awards from many significant organizations:

First Black Belt Magazine Cover	1966
Black Belt Hall of Fame Instructors Award	1969
Golden Fist Outstanding Official Award	1973
Black Belt Hall of Fame Man of the Year Award	1975
Four Seasons Award Outstanding Martial Artist	1981
US Congressional Distinguished Service Award	1984
Zendo-Kai Martial Artists Association Hall of Fame	1986
Cystic Fibrosis Foundation Volunteer Service Award	1987
California Secretary Award by March Fong Eu	1989
Huesped de Honor by the President of Guatemala	1990
Golden Masters Best Instructor Award	1993
State of Kentucky Colonel Award	1995
Award of Recognition by California Governor Pete Wilson	1995
20th Century Masters of Martial Arts	1998
World Martial Arts Hall of Fame	
· Most Distinguished Martial Artist Award	2000
· Golden Life Achievement Award (Excellence in Pioneering)	2000
National Association of Professional Martial Artists	
· Lifetime Achievement Award	2000
United States Karate Alliance	
· Black Belt Hall of Fame Award	2000
Special Recognition from the US Olympic Committee	2000
Black Belt Lifetime Achievement Award (Black Belt Magazine)	2000
California Police/Fire Games Appreciation Award	2001
Award of Recognition by US National Karate Federation	2001
Dragonfest Martial Art Hall of Fame Lifetime Achievement Award	2002
Budo Koroshoo – Japanese Imperial Honor Award	2002
US Martial Arts Hall of Fame Most Distinguished Karate Legend	2003
Living Regency Award, Florida	2005
World Martial Arts Hall of Fame Lifetime Achievement Award	2005
American Karate Association Hall of Fame	2008
Arnold Schwartzenegger's Lifetime Achievement Award	2008
World Martial Arts Masters Association Grandmaster	2008
Zenbei Butoku-Kai Lifetime Dedication Award	2009
USKA Lifetime Achievement Award	2011
Fumio Demura Day Martial Arts Museum of Los Angeles	2012
USA Martial Arts Hall of Fame	2013
Pro Tae Kwan Do Association Hall of Fame	2016
City of Santa Ana Award	2017
Fumio Demura Day Martial Arts Museum of Los Angeles	2017
OSKA Lifetime Achievement Award	2017

Mr. Demura has received letters of recognition from many important persons:

President of Guatemala Alvaro Arzu   1980
Governor of California Pete Wilson   1995
United States Senator from California Barbara Boxer   1995
President of the United States Bill Clinton   1996
President of the United States George Bush   2005
United States Senator from Rhode Island Kevin Breene   2005
Governor of California Arnold Schwarzenegger   2005
Governor of California Arnold Schwarzenegger   2010
President of the United States Barack Obama   2010
Senator of Hawaii Daniel Inouye   2011
Mayor of City of Winona, MN Jerry Miller   2012
City of Los Angeles Nisei Week, Eric Garcetti   2013
County of Los Angeles Board of Supervisors Michael Antonovich 2013
California State Legislature Assemblyman Donald Wagner   2013
City of Santa Ana Mayor Miguel Pulido   2015
County of Orange Board of Supervisors Andrew Do   2015
California State Legislature Assemblyman Tom Daly   2015

Mr. Demura participated in different ways in these productions:

Film Work

Rising Sun
Karate Kid (I [1984], II, III)
The Island of Dr. Moreau (1977)
Showdown in Little Tokyo
The Next Karate Kid
Mortal Kombat
Bad News Bears Go To Japan
The Nude Bomb
Blood and Bone
Shootfighter
Back Alley Princess (Hong Kong)
Ninja (2009) Nu-Image
The Real Miyagi (2015)

Television Work

O'Hara Series
Power Rangers
Space Rangers
Hocus Pocus
Warrior Within
Merv Griffin Show
Grey Hound
Mike Douglas Show
Joanne Worley Special
Don Francisco Show (Chile)
Puerto Rico Interview Show
20th Century Martial Arts
Call Me Bruce
Tempo
Karate-Kung-Fu Self Defense

Martial Arts in America
California Life Style
Hollywood Senichiya (Japan)
Martial Arts Today
Thicke of the Night
Sabado Gigante (Mexico)
Bring 'Em Back Alive
Dora's World
BBC Martial Arts Special
A&E - Samurai
A&E - Martial Arts
India TV Martial Arts Special
Walker Texas Ranger
BBC Northwest Show

Sekai O Kaeru 100 Nin No Nihonjim -
Tokyo TV (100 Japanese People Change the World)

Extreme Martial Arts - Discovery Channel
Modern Warriors, The Martial Way
History of Samurai - History Channel
TBS Japan Wow Wow "Best Kid"
Japanese Television "Nice to Meet You"
Ines Sanchez de Revuelta Show (Costa Rica) (3 years)